THE
MONKEY'S PAW

A STORY IN THREE SCENES

L 42

By
W. W. JACOBS

Dramatised by
LOUIS N. PARKER

New York SAMUEL FRENCH PUBLISHER 25 WEST 45TH STREET	London SAMUEL FRENCH, Ltd. 26 SOUTHAMPTON STREET STRAND

Produced at the Haymarket Theatre, London, on October 6, 1903, with the following cast :—

MR. WHITE	Mr. Cyril Maude.
MRS. WHITE	Miss Lena Ashwell.
HERBERT	Mr. Wilfred Forster.
SERGEANT-MAJOR MORRIS . .	Mr. Sydney Valentine.
MR. SAMPSON	Mr. Rudge Harding.

THE MONKEY'S PAW

SCENE.—*The living-room of an old-fashioned cottage on the outskirts of Fulham. Set corner-wise in the left angle at the back a deep window ; further front, L., three or four steps lead up to a door. Further forward a dresser, with plates, glasses, etc. R.C. at back an alcove with the street door fully visible. On the inside of the street door, a wire letter-box. On the right a cupboard, then a fireplace. In the centre a round table. Against the wall, L. back, an old-fashioned piano. A comfortable armchair each side of the fireplace. Other chairs. On the mantelpiece a clock, old china figures, etc. An air of comfort pervades the room.*

I

[*At the rise of the curtain,* MRS. WHITE, *a pleasant-looking old woman, is seated in the armchair below the fire, attending to a kettle which is steaming on the fire, and keeping a laughing eye on* MR. WHITE *and* HERBERT. *These two are seated at the right angle of the table nearest the fire with a chess-board between them.* MR. WHITE *is evidently losing. His hair is ruffled ; his spectacles are high up on his forehead.* HERBERT, *a fine young fellow, is looking with satisfaction at the move he has just made.* MR. WHITE *makes several attempts to move, but thinks*

better of them. There is a shaded lamp on the table.
The door is tightly shut. The curtains of the window
are drawn; but every now and then the wind is
heard whistling outside.)

MR. WHITE (*moving at last, and triumphant*).
There, Herbert, my boy! Got you, I think.

HERBERT. Oh, you're a deep 'un, dad, aren't you?

MRS. WHITE. Mean to say he's beaten you at
last?

HERBERT. Lor, no! Why, he's overlooked——

MR. WHITE (*very excited*). I see it! Lemme have
that back!

HERBERT. Not much. Rules of the game!

MR. WHITE (*disgusted*). I don't hold with them
scientific rules. You turn what ought to be an
innocent relaxation——

MRS. WHITE. Don't talk so much, father. You
put him off——

HERBERT (*laughing*). Not he!

MR. WHITE (*trying to distract his attention*). Hark
at the wind.

HERBERT (*drily*). Ah! I'm listening. Check.

MR. WHITE (*still trying to distract him*). I should
hardly think Sergeant-Major Morris'd come to-night.

HERBERT. Mate. (*Rises, goes up L.*)

MR. WHITE (*with an outbreak of disgust and sweep-
ing the chessmen off the board*). That's the worst of
living so far out. Your friends can't come for a
quiet chat, and you addle your brains over a con-
founded——

HERBERT. Now, father! Morris'll turn up all
right.

MR. WHITE (*still in a temper*). Lovers' Lane, Fulham! Ho! of all the beastly, slushy, out-o'-the-
way places to live in—— ! Pathway's a bog, and the
road's a torrent. (*To MRS. WHITE, who has risen, and
is at his side.*) What's the County Council thinking
of, that's what I want to know? Because this is the

only house in the road it doesn't matter if nobody can get near it, I s'pose.

MRS. WHITE. Never mind, dear. Perhaps you'll win to-morrow. (*She moves to back of table.*)

MR. WHITE. Perhaps I'll—perhaps I'll——! What d'you mean? (*Bursts out laughing.*) There! You always know what's going on inside o' me, don't you, mother?

MRS. WHITE. Ought to, after thirty years, John. (*She goes to dresser, and busies herself wiping tumblers on tray there.*)

(*He rises, goes to fireplace and lights pipe.*)

HERBERT (*down* C.). And it's not such a bad place, dad, after all. One of the few old-fashioned houses left near London. None o' your stucco villas. Home-like, I call it. And so do you, or you wouldn't ha' bought it. (*Rolls a cigarette.*)

MR. WHITE (R., *growling*). Nice job I made o' that, too! With two hundred pounds owin' on it.

HERBERT (*on back of chair*, C.). Why, I shall work that off in no time, dad. Matter o' three years, with the rise promised me.

MR. WHITE. If you don't get married.

HERBERT. Not me. Not that sort.

MRS. WHITE. I wish you would, Herbert. A good, steady, lad——

(*She brings the tray with a bottle of whisky, glasses, a lemon, spoons, buns, and a knife to the table.*)

HERBERT. Lots o' time, mother. Sufficient for the day—as the sayin' goes. Just now my dynamos don't leave me any time for love-making. Jealous they are, I tell you!

MR. WHITE (*chuckling*). I lay awake o' night often, and think: If Herbert took a nap, and let his what-d'you-call-ums—dynamos, run down, all Fulham would be in darkness. Lord ! what a joke ! (*gets* **R. C.**)

HERBERT. Joke ! And me with the sack ! Pretty idea of a joke you've got, I don't think.

(*Knock at outer door.*)

MRS. WHITE. Hark !

(*Knock repeated, louder.*)

MR. WHITE (*going towards door*). That's him. That's the Sergeant-Major. (*He unlocks door, back.*)

HERBERT (*removes chess-board*). Wonder what yarn he's got for us to-night. (*Places chess-board on piano.*)

MRS. WHITE (*goes up right, busies himself putting the other armchair nearer fire, etc.*). Don't let the door slam, John !

(MR. WHITE *opens the door a little, struggling with it. Wind.* SERGEANT-MAJOR MORRIS, *a veteran with a distinct military appearance—left arm gone— dressed as a commissionaire, is seen to enter.* MR. WHITE *helps him off with his coat, which he hangs up in the outer hall.*)

MR. WHITE (*at the door*). Slip in quick ! It's as much as I can do to hold it against the wind.

SERGEANT. Awful ! Awful ! (*Busy taking off his cloak, etc.*) And a mile up the road—by the ceme- tery—it's worse. Enough to blow the hair off your head.

MR. WHITE. Give me your stick.

SERGEANT. If 'twasn't I knew what a welcome I'd get——

MR. WHITE (*preceding him into the room*). Sergeant- Major Morris !

MRS. WHITE. Tut ! tut ! So cold you must be ! Come to the fire ; do'ee, now.

SERGEANT. How are you, marm ? (*To* HERBERT.) How's yourself, laddie ? Not on duty yet, eh ? Day-week, eh ?

HERBERT. (C.). No sir. Night week. But there's half an hour yet.

SERGEANT (*sitting in the armchair above the fire, which* MRS. WHITE *is motioning him towards*).

(MR. WHITE *mixes grog for* MORRIS.)

Thank'ee kindly, marm. That's good—hah ! That's a sight better than the trenches at Chitral. That's better than settin' in a puddle with the rain pourin' down in buckets, and the natives takin' pot-shots at you.

MRS. WHITE. Didn't you have no umbrellas ? (*Corner below fire, kneels before it, stirs it, etc.*)

SERGEANT. Umbrell——? Ho ! ho ! That's good ! Eh, White ? That's good. Did ye hear what she said ? Umbrellas !— *And* goloshes ! *and* hot-water bottles !—Ho, yes ! No offence, marm, but it's easy to see you was never a soldier.

HERBERT (*rather hurt*). Mother spoke out o' kindness, sir.

SERGEANT. And well I know it ; and no offence intended. No, marm, 'ardship, 'ardship is the soldier's lot. Starvation, fever, and get yourself shot. That's a bit o' my own.

MRS. WHITE. You don't look to've taken much harm—except—— (*Indicates his empty sleeve. She takes kettle to table, then returns to fire.*)

SERGEANT (*showing a medal hidden under his coat*). And that I got this for. No, marm. Tough. Thomas Morris is tough.

(MR. WHITE *is holding a glass of grog under the* SERGEANT'S *nose.*)

And sober. What's this now ?

MR. WHITE. Put your nose in it; you'll see.

SERGEANT. Whisky? And hot? And sugar? And a slice o' lemon? No. I said I'd never—but seein' the sort o' night. Well! (*Waving the glass at them.*) Here's another thousand a year!

MR. WHITE (*sits R. of table, also with a glass*). Same to you, and many of 'em.

SERGEANT (*to* HERBERT, *who has no glass*). What? Not you?

HERBERT (*laughing and sitting across chair,* C.). Oh! 'tisn't for want of being sociable. But my work don't go with it. Not if 'twas ever so little. I've got to keep a cool head, a steady eye, and a still hand. The fly-wheel might gobble me up.

MRS. WHITE. Don't, Herbert. (*Sits in armchair below fire.*)

HERBERT (*laughing*). No fear, mother.

SERGEANT. Ah! you electricians!—Sort o' magicians, you are. Light! says you—and light it is. And, power! says you—and the trams go whizzin'. And, knowledge! says you—and words go 'ummin' to the ends o' the world. It fair beats me—and I've seen a bit in my time, too.

HERBERT (*nudges his father*). Your Indian magic? All a fake, governor. The fakir's fake.

SERGEANT. Fake. you call it? I tell you, I've *seen* it.

HERBERT (*nudging his father with his foot*). Oh, come, now! such as what? Come, now!

SERGEANT. I've seen a cove with no more clothes on than a babby, (*to* MRS. WHITE) if you know what I mean—take an empty basket—empty, mind!—as empty as—as this here glass——

MR. WHITE. Hand it over, Morris. (*Hands it to* HERBERT, *who goes quickly behind table and fills it.*)

SERGEANT. Which was not my intentions, but used for illustration.

HERBERT (*while mixing*). Oh, *I've* seen the basket trick! and I've read how it was done. Why, I

could do it myself, with a bit o' practice. Ladle
out something stronger.

(HERBERT *brings him the glass.*)

SERGEANT. Stronger ?—what do you say to an
old fakir chuckin' a rope up in the air—in the *air,*
mind you !—and swarming up it, same as if it was
'ooked on—and vanishing clean out o' sight ?—I've
seen *that.*

(HERBERT *goes to table, plunges a knife into a bun and
offers it to the* SERGEANT *with exaggerated polite-
ness.*)

SERGEANT (*eyeing it with disgust*). Bun— ? What
for ?
HERBERT. That yarn takes it.

(MR. *and* MRS. WHITE *delighted.*)

SERGEANT. Mean to say you doubt my word ?
MRS. WHITE. No, no ! He's only taking you
off.—You shouldn't, Herbert.
MR. WHITE. Herbert always was one for a bit o'
fun !

(HERBERT *puts bun back on table, comes round in front,
and moving the chair out of the way, sits cross-legged
on the floor at his father's side.*)

SERGEANT. But it's true. Why, if I chose, I
could tell you things—— But there ! you don't get
no more yarns out o' *me.*
MR. WHITE. Nonsense, old friend. (*Puts down his
glass.*) You're not going to get shirty about a bit
o' fun. (*Moves his chair nearer* MORRIS's.) What
was that you started telling me the other day about
a monkey's paw, or something ? (*Nudges* HERBERT,
and winks at MRS. WHITE.)

SERGEANT (*gravely*). Nothing. Leastways, nothing worth hearing.

MRS. WHITE (*with astonished curiosity*). Monkey's paw——?

MR. WHITE. Ah—you was tellin' me——

SERGEANT. Nothing. Don't go on about it. (*Puts his empty glass to his lips—then stares at it.*) What? Empty again? There! When I begin thinkin' o' the paw, it makes me that absent-minded——

MR. WHITE (*rises and fills glass*). You said you always carried it on you.

SERGEANT. So I do, for fear o' what might happen. (*Sunk in thought.*) Ay!—ay!

MR. WHITE (*handing him his glass refilled*). There. (*Sits again in same chair.*)

MRS. WHITE. What's it for?

SERGEANT. You wouldn't believe me, if I was to tell you.

HERBERT. *I* will, every word.

SERGEANT. Magic, then!—Don't you laugh!

HERBERT. I'm not. Got it on you now?

SERGEANT. Of course.

HERBERT. Let's see it.

(*Seeing the* SERGEANT *embarrassed with his glass,* MRS. WHITE *rises, takes it from him, places it on mantelpiece and remains standing.*)

SERGEANT. Oh, it's nothing to look at. (*Hunting in his pocket.*) Just an ordinary—little paw—dried to a mummy. (*Produces it and holds it towards* MRS. WHITE.) Here.

MRS. WHITE (*who has leant forward eagerly to see it, starts back with a little cry of disgust*). Oh!

HERBERT. Give us a look. (MORRIS *passes the paw to* MR. WHITE, *from whom* HERBERT *takes it.*) Why, it's all dried up!

SERGEANT. I said so.

(*Wind.*)

MRS. WHITE (*with a slight shudder*). Hark at the wind! (*Sits again in her old place.*)

MR. WHITE (*taking the paw from* HERBERT). And what might there be special about it?

SERGEANT (*impressively*). That there paw has had a spell put upon it!

MR. WHITE. No? (*In great alarm he thrusts the paw back into* MORRIS'S *hand.*)

SERGEANT (*pensively, holding the paw in the palm of his hand*). Ah! By an old fakir. He was a very holy man. He'd sat all doubled up in one spot, goin' on for fifteen year; thinkin' o' things. And he wanted to show that fate ruled people. That everything was cut and dried from the beginning, as you might say. That there warn't no gettin' away from it. And that, if you tried to, you caught it hot. (*Pauses solemnly.*) So he put a spell on this bit of a paw. It might ha' been anything else, but he took the first thing that came handy. Ah! He put a spell on it, and made it so that three people (*looking at them and with deep meaning*) could each have three wishes.

(*All but* MRS. WHITE *laugh rather nervously.*)

MRS. WHITE. Ssh! Don't!

SERGEANT (*more gravely*). But——! But, mark you, though the wishes was granted, those three people would have cause to wish they *hadn't* been.

MR. WHITE. But how *could* the wishes be granted?

SERGEANT. He didn't say. It would all happen so natural, you might think it a coincidence if so disposed.

HERBERT. Why haven't you tried it, sir?

SERGEANT (*gravely, after a pause*). I have.

HERBERT (*eagerly*). You've had your three wishes?

SERGEANT (*gravely*). Yes.

MRS. WHITE. Were they granted?

SERGEANT (*staring at the fire*).   They were.

(*A pause.*)

MR. WHITE. Has anybody else wished ?

SERGEANT.   Yes. The first owner had his **three** wish—— (*Lost in recollection.*) Yes, oh yes, he had his three wishes all right. I don't know what his first two were, (*very impressively*) but the third was for death. (*All shudder.*) That's how I got the paw.

(*A pause.*)

HERBERT (*cheerfully*). Well ! Seems to me you've only got to wish for things that *can't* have any bad luck about 'em—— (*Rises.*)

SERGEANT (*shaking his head*). Ah !

MR. WHITE (*tentatively*). Morris—if you've had your three wishes—it's no good to you, now—what do you keep it for ?

SERGEANT (*still holding the paw; looking at it*). Fancy, I s'pose. I did have some idea of selling it, but I don't think I will. It's done mischief enough already. Besides, people won't buy. Some of 'em think it's a fairy tale. And some want to try it first, and pay after.

(*Nervous laugh from the others.*)

MRS. WHITE. If you could have another **three** wishes, would you ?

SERGEANT (*slowly—weighing the paw in his hand, and looking at it*). I don't know—I don't know—— (*Suddenly, with violence, flinging it in the fire.*) No ! I'm damned if I would !

(*Movement from all.*)

MR. WHITE (*rises and quickly snatches it out of the fire*). What are you doing ?

(WHITE *goes* R. C.)

SERGEANT (*rising and following him and trying to*

prevent him). Let it burn! Let the infernal thing burn!

MRS. WHITE (*rises*). Let it burn, father!

MR. WHITE (*wiping it on his coat-sleeve*). No. If you don't want it, give it to me.

SERGEANT (*violently*). I won't! I won't! My hands are clear of it. I threw it on the fire. If you keep it, don't blame me, whatever happens. Here! Pitch it back again.

MR. WHITE (*stubbornly*). I'm going to keep it. What do you say, Herbert?

HERBERT (L. C., *laughing*). I say, keep it if you want to. Stuff and nonsense, anyhow.

MR. WHITE (*looking at the paw thoughtfully*). Stuff and nonsense. Yes. I wonder—(*casually*) I wish—— (*He was going to say some ordinary thing, like " I wish I were certain."*)

SERGEANT (*misunderstanding him ; violently*). Stop! Mind what you're doing. That's not the way.

MR. WHITE. What *is* the way?

MRS. WHITE (*moving away, up* R.C. *to back of table, and beginning to put the tumblers straight, and the chairs in their places*). Oh, don't have anything to do with it, John.

(*Takes glasses on tray to dresser,* L., *busies herself there, rinsing them in a bowl of water on the dresser, and wiping them with a cloth.*)

SERGEANT. That's what I say, marm. But if I warn't to tell him, he might go wishing something he didn't mean to. You hold it in your right hand, and wish aloud. But I warn you! I warn you!

MRS. WHITE. Sounds like the Arabian Nights. Don't you think you might wish me four pair o' hands?

MR. WHITE (*laughing*). Right you are, mother!— I wish——

SERGEANT (*pulling his arm down*). Stop it! If you must wish, wish for something sensible. Look

here! **I** can't stand this. Gets on my nerves. Where's my coat ? (*Goes into alcove.*)

(MR. WHITE *crosses to fireplace and carefully puts the paw on mantelpiece. He is absorbed in it to the end of the tableau.*)

HERBERT.   I'm coming your way, to the works, in a minute. Won't you wait ? (*Goes up* C., *helps* MORRIS *with his coat.*)

SERGEANT (*putting on his coat.*)   No. I'm all shook up. I want fresh air. I don't want to be here when you wish. And wish you will as soon's my back's turned. I know. I know. But I've warned you, mind.

MR. WHITE (*helping him into his coat*).   All right, Morris. Don't you fret about us. (*Gives him money.*) Here.

SERGEANT (*refusing it*).   No, I won't——

MR. WHITE (*forcing it into his hand*).   Yes, you will (*Opens door.*)

SERGEANT (*turning to the room*).   Well, good-night all. (*To* WHITE.)   Put it in the fire.

ALL.   Good-night.

(*Exit* SERGEANT.   MR. WHITE *closes door, comes towards fireplace, absorbed in the paw.*)

HERBERT (*down* L.).   If there's no more in this than there is in his other stories, we shan't make much out of it.

MRS. WHITE (*comes down* R. C. *to* WHITE).   Did you give him anything for it, father ?

MR. WHITE.   A trifle. He didn't want it, but I made him take it.

MRS. WHITE.   There, now! You shouldn't. Throwing your money about.

MR. WHITE (*looking at the paw which he has picked up again*).   I wonder——

HERBERT.   What ?

MR. WHITE. I wonder, whether we hadn't better chuck it on the fire ?

HERBERT (*laughing*). Likely ! Why, we're all going to be rich and famous, and happy.

MRS. WHITE. Throw it on the fire, indeed, when you've given money for it ! So like you, father.

HERBERT. Wish to be an Emperor, father, to begin with. Then you can't be henpecked !

MRS. WHITE (*going for him front of table with a duster*). You young—— ! (*Follows him to back of table.*)

HERBERT (*running away from her round behind table*). Steady with that duster, mother !

MR. WHITE. Be quiet, there ! (HERBERT *catches* MRS. WHITE *in his arms and kisses her.*) I wonder—— (*He has the paw in his hand.*) I don't know what to wish for, and that's a fact. (*He looks about him with a happy smile.*) I seem to've got all I want.

HERBERT (*with his hands on the old man's shoulders*). Old dad ! If you'd only cleared the debt on the house, you'd be quite happy, wouldn't you ? (*Laughing.*) Well—go ahead !—wish for the two hundred pounds : that'll just do it.

MR. WHITE (*half laughing*). Shall I ?

(*Crosses to* R. C.)

HERBERT. Go on ! Here !—I'll play slow music. (*Crosses to piano.*)

MRS. WHITE. Don't 'ee, John. Don't have nothing to do with it !

HERBERT. Now, dad ! (*Plays.*)

MR. WHITE. I will ! (*Holds up the paw, as if half ashamed.*) I wish for two hundred pounds.

(*Crash on the piano. At the same instant* MR. WHITE *utters a cry and lets the paw drop.*)

MRS. WHITE
    and   } What's the matter ?
HERBERT.

MR. WHITE (*gazing with horror at the paw*). It moved ! As I wished, it twisted in my hand like a snake.

HERBERT (*goes down* R., *and picks the paw up*). Nonsense, dad. Why, it's as stiff as a bone. (*Lays it on the mantelpiece.*)

MRS. WHITE. Must have been your fancy, father,

HERBERT (*laughing*). Well——? (*Looking round the room.*) I don't see the money ; and I bet I never shall.

MR. WHITE (*relieved*). Thank God, there's no harm done ! But it gave me a shock.

HERBERT. Half-past eleven. I must get along. I'm on at midnight. (*Goes up* C., *fetches his coat, etc.*) We've had quite a merry evening.

MRS. WHITE. I'm off to bed. Don't be late for breakfast, Herbert.

HERBERT. I shall walk home as usual. Does me good. I shall be with you about nine. Don't wait, though.

MRS. WHITE. You know your father never waits.

HERBERT. Good-night, mother. (*Kisses her. She lights candle on dresser*, L., *goes up stairs and exit.*)

HERBERT (*coming to his father*, R., *who is sunk in thought*). Good-night, dad. You'll find the cash tied up in the middle of the bed.

MR. WHITE (*staring, seizes* HERBERT'S *hand*). It moved, Herbert.

HERBERT. Ah ! And a monkey hanging by his tail from the bed-post, watching you count the golden sovereigns.

MR. WHITE (*accompanying him to the door*). I wish you wouldn't joke, my boy.

HERBERT. All right, dad. (*Opens door.*) Lord ! What weather ! Good-night. (*Exit.*)

(*The old man shakes his head, closes the door, locks it, puts the chain up, slips the lower bolt, has some difficulty with the upper bolt.*)

MR. WHITE. This bolt's stiff again! I must get Herbert to look to it in the morning.

(Comes into the room, puts out the lamp, crosses towards steps ; but is irresistibly attracted towards fireplace. Sits down and stares into the fire. His expression changes : he sees something horrible.)

MR. WHITE *(with an involuntary cry)*. Mother! Mother!

MRS. WHITE *(appearing at the door at the top of the steps with candle)*. What's the matter? *(Comes down R. C.)*

MR. WHITE *(mastering himself. Rises)*. Nothing —I—haha!—I saw faces in the fire.

MRS. WHITE. Come along.

(She takes his arm and draws him towards the steps. He looks back frightened towards fireplace as they reach the first step.)

TABLEAU CURTAIN.

II

(*Bright sunshine. The table, which has been moved nearer the window, is laid for breakfast. MRS. WHITE busy about the table. MR. WHITE standing in the window looking off R. The inner door is open, showing the outer door.*)

MR. WHITE. What a morning Herbert's got for walking home !

MRS. WHITE (L. C.). What's o'clock ? (*Looks at clock on mantelpiece.*) Quarter to nine, I declare. He's off at eight. (*Crosses to fire.*)

MR. WHITE. Takes him half-an-hour to change and wash. He's just by the cemetery now.

MRS. WHITE. He'll be here in ten minutes.

MR. WHITE (*coming to the table*). What's for breakfast ?

MRS. WHITE. Sausages. (*At the mantelpiece.*) Why, if here isn't that dirty monkey's paw ! (*Picks it up, looks at it with disgust, puts it back. Takes sausages in dish from before fire and places them on table.*) Silly thing ! The idea of us listening to such nonsense !

MR. WHITE (*goes up to window again*). Ay—the Sergeant-Major and his yarns ! I suppose all old soldiers are alike——

MRS. WHITE. Come on, father. Herbert hates us to wait.

(*They both sit and begin breakfast.*)

MRS. WHITE. How could wishes be granted, now-adays ?

MR. WHITE. Ah! Been thinking about it all night, have you?

MRS. WHITE. You kept me awake, with your tossing and tumbling——

MR. WHITE. Ay, I had a bad night.

MRS. WHITE. It was the storm, I expect. How it blew!

MR. WHITE. I didn't hear it. I was asleep and not asleep, if you know what I mean.

MRS. WHITE. And all that rubbish about its making you unhappy if your wish *was* granted! How could two hundred pounds hurt you, eh, father?

MR. WHITE. Might drop on my head in a lump. Don't see any other way. And I'd try to bear that. Though, mind you, Morris said it would all happen so naturally that you might take it for a coincidence, if so disposed.

MRS. WHITE. Well—it hasn't happened. That's all I know. And it isn't going to. (*A letter is seen to drop in the letter-box.*) And how you can sit there and talk about it—— (*Sharp postman's knock; she jumps to her feet.*) What's that?

MR. WHITE. Postman, o' course.

MRS. WHITE (*seeing the letter from a distance; in an awed whisper*). He's brought a letter, John!

MR. WHITE (*laughing*). What did you think he'd bring? Ton o' coals?

MRS. WHITE. John—! John—! Suppose——?

MR. WHITE. Suppose what?

MRS. WHITE. Suppose it was two hundred pounds!

MR. WHITE (*suppressing his excitement*). Eh!— Here! Don't talk nonsense. Why don't you fetch it?

MRS. WHITE (*crosses and takes letter out of the box*). It's thick, John—(*feels it*)—and—and it's got something crisp inside it. (*Takes letter to* WHITE, R. C.)

MR. WHITE. Who—who's it for?

MRS. WHITE. You.

MR. WHITE. Hand it over, then. (*Feeling and examining it with ill-concealed excitement.*) The idea! What a superstitious old woman you are! Where are my specs?

MRS. WHITE. Let me open it.

MR. WHITE. Don't you touch it. Where are my specs?

(*Goes to* R.)

MRS. WHITE. Don't let sudden wealth sour your temper, John.

MR. WHITE. *Will* you find my specs?

MRS. WHITE (*taking them off mantelpiece*). Here, John, here.

(*As he opens the letter.*)

Take care! Don't tear it!

MR. WHITE. Tear what?

MRS. WHITE. If it was banknotes, John!

MR. WHITE (*taking a thick, formal document out of the envelope and a crisp-looking slip*). You've gone dotty.—You've made me nervous. (*Reads.*) "Sir,— Enclosed please find receipt for interest on the mortgage of £200 on your house, duly received."

(*They look at each other.* MR. WHITE *sits down to finish his breakfast silently.* MRS. WHITE *goes to the window.*)

MRS. WHITE. That comes of listening to tipsy old soldiers.

MR. WHITE (*pettish*). What does?

MRS. WHITE. You thought there was banknotes in it.

MR. WHITE (*injured*). I didn't! I said all along——

MRS. WHITE. How Herbert will laugh, when I tell him!

MR. WHITE (*with gruff good-humour*). You're not going to tell him. You're going to keep your mouth

shut. That's what you're going to do. Why, I should never hear the last of it.

MRS. WHITE. Serve you right. I shall tell him. You know you like his fun. See how he joked you last night when you said the paw moved.

(She is looking through the window towards R.*)*

MR. WHITE. So it did. It did move. That I'll swear to.

MRS. WHITE *(abstractedly: she is watching something outside).* You thought it did.

MR. WHITE. I say it did. There was no thinking about it. You saw how it upset me, didn't you?

(She doesn't answer.)

Didn't you?—Why don't you listen? *(Turns round.)* What is it?

MRS. WHITE. Nothing.

MR. WHITE *(turns back to his breakfast).* Do you see Herbert coming?

MRS. WHITE. No.

MR. WHITE. He's about due. What *is* it?

MRS. WHITE. Nothing. Only a man. Looks like a gentleman. Leastways, he's in black, and he's got a top-hat on.

MR. WHITE. What about him? *(He is not interested; goes on eating.)*

MRS. WHITE. He stood at the garden-gate as if he wanted to come in. But he couldn't seem to make up his mind.

MR. WHITE. Oh, go on! You're full o' fancies.

MRS. WHITE. He's going—no; he's coming back.

MR. WHITE. Don't let him see you peeping.

MRS. WHITE *(with increasing excitement).* He's looking at the house. He's got his hand on the latch.

No. He turns away again. (*Eagerly.*) John! He looks like a sort of a lawyer.

MR. WHITE.   What of it?

MRS. WHITE.   Oh, you'll only laugh again.   But suppose—suppose he's coming about the two hundred——

MR. WHITE.   You're not to mention it again!— You're a foolish old woman.—Come and eat your breakfast. (*Eagerly.*)   Where is he now?

MRS. WHITE.   Gone down the road.   He has turned back.   He seems to've made up his mind.   Here he comes!—Oh, John, and me all untidy! (*Crosses to fire* R.)

(*Knock.*)

MR. WHITE (*to* MRS. WHITE *who is hastily smoothing her hair, etc.*).   What's it matter?   He's made a mistake.   Come to the wrong house. (*Crosses to fireplace.*)

(MRS. WHITE *opens the door.* MR. SAMPSON, *dressed from head to foot in solemn black, with a top-hat, stands in the doorway.*)

SAMPSON (*outside*).   Is this Mr. White's?

MRS. WHITE.   Come in, sir.   Please step in.

(*She shows him into the room; goes* R., *he is awkward and nervous.*)

You must overlook our being so untidy; and the room all anyhow; and John in his garden-coat. (*To* MR. WHITE, *reproachfully*).   Oh, John.

SAMPSON (*to* MR. WHITE).   Morning.   My name is Sampson.

MRS. WHITE (*offering a chair*).   Won't you please be seated?

(SAMPSON *stands quite still up* C.)

SAMPSON. Ah—thank you—no, I think not—I think not. (*Pause.*)

MR. WHITE (*awkwardly, trying to help him*). Fine weather for the time o' year.

SAMPSON. Ah—yes—yes—— (*Pause ; he makes a renewed effort.*) My name is Sampson—I've come——

MRS. WHITE. Perhaps you was wishful to see Herbert ; he'll be home in a minute. (*Pointing.*) Here's his breakfast waiting——

SAMPSON (*interrupting her hastily*). No, no ! (*Pause.*) I've come from the electrical works——

MRS. WHITE. Why, you might have come with him.

(MR. WHITE *sees something is wrong, tenderly puts his hand on her arm.*)

SAMPSON. No—no—I've come—*alone.*

MRS. WHITE (*with a little anxiety*). Is anything the matter ?

SAMPSON. I was asked to call——

MRS. WHITE (*abruptly*). Herbert ! Has anything happened ? Is he hurt ? Is he hurt ?

MR. WHITE (*soothing her*). There, there, mother. Don't you jump to conclusions. Let the gentleman speak. You've not brought bad news, I'm sure, sir.

SAMPSON. I'm—sorry——

MRS. WHITE. Is he hurt ?

(SAMPSON *bows.*)

MRS. WHITE. Badly ?

SAMPSON. Very badly. (*Turns away.*)

MRS. WHITE (*with a cry*). John— ! (*She instinctively moves towards* WHITE.)

MR. WHITE. Is he in pain ?

SAMPSON. He is not in pain.

MRS. WHITE. Oh, thank God ! Thank God for

that ! Thank—— (*She looks in a startled fashion at* MR. WHITE—*realizes what* SAMPSON *means, catches his arm and tries to turn him towards her*). Do you mean—— ?

(SAMPSON *avoids her look; she gropes for her husband : he takes her two hands in his, and gently lets her sink into the armchair above the fireplace, then he stands on her right, between her and* SAMPSON.)

MR. WHITE (*hoarsely*). Go on, sir.
SAMPSON. He was telling his mates a story. Something that had happened here last night. He was laughing, and wasn't noticing and—and—(*hushed*) the machinery caught him——

(*A little cry from* MRS. WHITE, *her face shows her horror and agony.*)

MR. WHITE (*vague, holding* MRS. WHITE'S *hand*). The machinery caught him—yes—and him the only child—it's hard, sir—very hard——
SAMPSON (*subdued*). The Company wished me to convey their sincere sympathy with you in your great loss——
MR. WHITE (*staring blankly*). Our—great—loss—— !
SAMPSON. I was to say further—(*as if apologizing*) I am only their servant—I am only obeying orders——
MR. WHITE. Our—great—loss——
SAMPSON (*laying an envelope on the table and edging towards the door*). I was to say, the Company disclaim all responsibility, but, in consideration of your son's services, they wish to present you with a certain sum as compensation. (*Gets to door.*)
MR. WHITE. Our—great—loss—— (*Suddenly, with horror.*) How—how much ?

SAMPSON (*in the doorway*). Two hundred pounds.

(*Exit.*)

(MRS. WHITE *gives a cry. The old man takes no heed of her, smiles faintly, puts out his hands like a sightless man, and drops, a senseless heap, to the floor.* MRS. WHITE *stares at him blankly and her hands go out helplessly towards him.*)

TABLEAU CURTAIN.

III

(Night. On the table a candle is flickering at its last gasp. The room looks neglected. Mr. White *is dozing fitfully in the armchair.* Mrs. White *is in the window peering through the blind towards* L.*)*

(Mr. White *starts, wakes, looks around him.*)

Mr. White *(fretfully).* Jenny—Jenny.

Mrs. White *(in the window).* Yes.

Mr. White. Where are you?

Mrs. White. At the window.

Mr. White. What are you doing?

Mrs. White. Looking up the road.

Mr. White *(falling back).* What's the use, Jenny? What's the use?

Mrs. White. That's where the cemetery is; that's where we've laid him.

Mr. White. Ay—ay—a week to-day—what o'clock is it?

Mrs. White. I don't know.

Mr. White. We don't take much account of time now, Jenny, do we?

Mrs. White. Why should we? He don't come home. He'll never come home again. There's nothing to think about——

Mr. White. Or to talk about. *(Pause.)* Come away from the window; you'll get cold.

Mrs. White. It's colder where *he* is.

Mr. White. Ay—gone for ever——

MRS. WHITE. And taken all our hopes with him——

MR. WHITE. And all our *wishes*——

MRS. WHITE. Ay, and all our—— (*With a sudden cry.*) John !

(*She comes quickly to him ; he rises.*)

MR. WHITE. Jenny ! For God's sake ! What's the matter ?

MRS. WHITE (*with dreadful eagerness*). The *paw* ! The monkey's paw !

MR. WHITE (*bewildered*). Where ? Where is it ? What's wrong with it ?

MRS. WHITE. I want it ! You haven't done away with it ?

MR. WHITE. I haven't seen it—since—why ?

MRS. WHITE. I want it ! Find it ! Find it !

MR. WHITE (*groping on the mantelpiece*). Here ! Here it is ! What do you want of it ? (*He leaves it there.*)

MRS. WHITE. Why didn't I think of it ? Why didn't *you* think of it ?

MR. WHITE. Think of what ?

MRS. WHITE. The *other two* wishes !

MR. WHITE (*with horror*). What ?

MRS. WHITE. We've only had one.

MR. WHITE (*tragically*). Wasn't that enough ?

MRS. WHITE. No ! We'll have one more. (WHITE *crosses to* R. C. MRS. WHITE *takes the paw and follows him.*) Take it. Take it quickly. And wish——

MR. WHITE (*avoiding the paw*). Wish what ?

MRS. WHITE. Oh, John ! John ! Wish our boy alive again !

MR. WHITE. Good God ! Are you mad ?

MRS. WHITE. Take it. Take it and wish. (*With a paroxysm of grief.*) Oh, my boy ! My boy !

MR. WHITE. Get to bed. Get to sleep. You don't know what you're saying.

MRS. WHITE. We had the first wish granted—why not the second ?

MR. WHITE (*hushed*). He's been dead ten days, and—Jenny! Jenny! I only knew him by his clothing—if you wasn't allowed to see him then—how could you bear to see him *now* ?

MRS. WHITE. I don't care. Bring him back.

MR. WHITE (*shrinking from the paw*). I daren't touch it !

MRS. WHITE (*thrusting it in his hand*). Here ! Here ! Wish !

MR. WHITE (*trembling*). Jenny !

MRS. WHITE (*fiercely*). WISH. (*She goes on frantically whispering " Wish."*)

MR. WHITE (*shuddering, but overcome by her insistence*). I—I—wish—my—son—alive again.

(*He drops it with a cry. The candle goes out. Utter darkness. He sinks into a chair. MRS. WHITE hurries to the window and draws the blind back. She stands in the moonlight. Pause.*)

MRS. WHITE (*drearily*). Nothing.

MR. WHITE. Thank God ! Thank God !

MRS. WHITE. Nothing at all. Along the whole length of the road not a living thing. (*Closes blind.*) And nothing, nothing, nothing left in our lives, John.

MR. WHITE. Except each other, Jenny—and memories.

MRS. WHITE (*coming back slowly to the fireplace*). We're too old. We were only alive in him. We can't begin again. We can't feel anything now, John, but emptiness and darkness. (*She sinks into armchair.*)

MR. WHITE. 'Tisn't for long, Jenny. There's that to look forward to.

MRS. WHITE. Every minute's long, now.

MR. WHITE (*rising*). I can't bear the darkness !

MRS. WHITE. It's dreary—dreary.

MR. WHITE (*crosses to dresser*). Where's the candle ?

(*Finds it and brings it to table.*) And the matches ?
Where are the matches ? We mustn't sit in the dark.
'Tisn't wholesome. (*Lights match ; the other candle-
stick is close to him.*) There. (*Turning with the
lighted match towards* MRS. WHITE, *who is rocking and
moaning.*) Don't take on so, mother.

MRS. WHITE. I'm a mother no longer.

MR. WHITE (*lights candle*). There now ; there
now. Go on up to bed. Go on, now—I'm a-coming.

MRS. WHITE. Whether I'm here or in bed, or
wherever I am, I'm with my boy, I'm with——

(*A low single knock at the street door.*)

MRS. WHITE (*starting*). What's that !

MR. WHITE (*mastering his horror*). A rat. The
house is full of 'em.

(*A louder single knock ; she starts up. He catches her
by the arm.*)

Stop ! What are you going to do ?

MRS. WHITE (*wildly*). It's my boy ! It's Herbert !
I forgot it was a mile away ! What are you holding
me for ? I must open the door !

(*The knocking continues in single knocks at irregular
intervals, constantly growing louder and more insist-
ant.*)

MR. WHITE (*still holding her*). For God's sake !

MRS. WHITE (*struggling*). Let me go !

MR. WHITE. Don't open the door !

(*He drags her towards left front.*)

MRS. WHITE. Let me go !

MR. WHITE. Think what you might see !

MRS. WHITE (*struggling fiercely*). Do you think I fear the child I bore! Let me go! (*She wrenches herself loose and rushes to the door which she tears open.*) I'm coming, Herbert! I'm coming!

MR. WHITE (*cowering in the extreme corner, left front*). Don't 'ee do it! Don't 'ee do it!

(MRS. WHITE *is at work on the outer door, where the knocking still continues. She slips the chain, slips the lower bolt, unlocks the door.*)

MR. WHITE (*suddenly*). The paw! Where's the monkey's paw?

(*He gets on his knees and feels along the floor for it.*)

MRS. WHITE (*tugging at the top bolt*). John! The top bolt's stuck. I can't move it. Come and help. Quick!

MR. WHITE (*wildly groping*). The paw! Ther s a wish left.

(*The knocking is now loud, and in groups of increasing length between the speeches.*)

MRS. WHITE. D'ye hear him? John! Your child's knocking!

MR. WHITE. Where is it? Where did it fall?

MRS. WHITE (*tugging desperately at the bolt*). Help! Help! Will you keep your child from his home?

MR. WHITE. Where did it fall? I can't find it— I can't find——

(*The knocking is now tempestuous, and there are blows upon the door as of a body beating against it.*)

MRS. WHITE. Herbert! Herbert! My boy! Wait! Your mother's opening to you! Ah! It's moving! It's moving!

MR. WHITE. God forbid! (*Finds the paw.*) Ah!

MRS. WHITE (*slipping the bolt*). Herbert!

MR. WHITE (*has raised himself to his knees; he holds the paw high*). I wish him dead. (*The knocking stops abruptly.*) I wish him dead and at peace!

MRS. WHITE (*flinging the door open simultaneously*). Herb——

(*A flood of moonlight. Emptiness. The old man sways in prayer on his knees. The old woman lies half swooning, wailing against the door-post.*)

CURTAIN.

BACK-CLOTH—COUNTRY LANE OR GARDEN CLOTH.

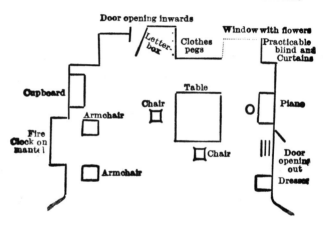